China Impressions
The Beauty of Yunnan

中国印象
大美云南

五洲传播出版社
China Intercontinental Press

Mountains and Canyons
高山峡谷
雪域王国

Yulong Snow Mountain
1 / 玉龙雪山

Meili Snow Mountain
2 / 梅里雪山

Hutiao Gorge
3 / 虎跳峡

Grand Canyon of the Nujiang River
4 / 怒江大峡谷

Three Parallel Rivers
5 / 三江并流

The Realm of Mortals and the Celestial Paradise
人间仙境
世外桃源

Lugu Lake
6 / 泸沽湖

Xishuangbanna
7 / 西双版纳

Shangri-La
8 / 香格里拉

Yuanyang Rice Terraces
9 / 元阳梯田

Dongchuan Red Land
10 / 东川红土地

Dawn and Dusk in the Ancient Cities
古城晨昏

人间烟火

Kunming
11 / 昆明

The Ancient City of Dali
12 / 大理古城

Dayan Ancient Town
13 / 大研古镇

Dukezong
14 / 独克宗

Heshun
15 / 和顺

Historical Relics and Cultural Heritage
古迹人文

精神家园

NSAU Bookstore of Librairie Avant-Garde
16 / 西南联大先锋书店

Yunnan Provincial Museum
17 / 云南省博物馆

Ganden Sumtseling Monastery
18 / 噶丹松赞林寺

Three Pagodas of Chongsheng Temple
19 / 崇圣寺三塔

Yunnan Ethnic Village
20 / 云南民族村

Mountains and Canyons

高山峡谷 雪域王国

Yulong Snow Mountain

A Snowy Wonderland of Exotic Flowers and Rare Plants

玉龙雪山 | 奇花异草的雪域王国

Amidst the lush, vibrant greenery of the spruce meadow, Yulong Snow Mountain gleams with a cold, piercing brilliance under the sunlight. In the distance, 13 snow-capped peaks stretch from south to north, resembling a majestic "giant dragon" in all its awe-inspiring grandeur. In the Naxi language, Yulong Snow Mountain is referred to as the "Heavenly Mountain." The mountain's composition of limestone and basalt creates a striking contrast of black and white, earning it the moniker "Black and White Snow Mountain." The highest peak, Shanzi ("Fan") Peak, rises to an elevation of 5,596 meters, making it the closest snow-capped mountain to the equator in the Northern Hemisphere.

穿过云杉坪密密匝匝的耀眼绿色，玉龙雪山在阳光之下闪烁着冷冽光芒。远处，十三座雪峰从南向北纵向排列，宛若一条“巨龙”奔腾而去，壮观威武。玉龙雪山在纳西语中意为“天山”，山上岩性为石灰岩与玄武岩，黑白相间分明，故而又被称为“黑白雪山”，主峰扇子陡最高海拔 5596 米，是北半球最近赤道终年积雪的山脉。

Meili Snow Mountain

A Celestial Sanctuary Guarded by Kawakarpo Peak

梅里雪山 | 卡瓦格博守护的雪山仙境

Before dawn, Feilai Temple, nestled at the foot of the snow-capped mountains, is just a faint silhouette in the early morning light. As the sun rises, its rays reveal the sharp peak of Kawakarpo emerging from a drifting sea of clouds. Meili Snow Mountain, straddling the border between Yunnan and Xizang within the Hengduan Mountains, is crowned by 13 peaks, each averaging over 6,000 meters in elevation, collectively known as the "Thirteen Peaks of the Prince." The main peak, Kawakarpo, stands at an elevation of 6,740 meters, and is revered by the Xizang people as the deity of the snow mountains. Meili Snow Mountain's treasures include its dense forests, lush meadows, majestic glaciers, and rare flora. To this day, Meili Snow Mountain remains a pristine, virgin peak, unconquered by human ascent.

黎明前，雪山脚下的飞来寺还是晨光中一片依稀的黑影。伴随着霞光万道的，是漂浮不定的云海中卡瓦格博的凌厉峰顶。梅里雪山，是横断山脉滇藏边界上南北走向的雪山群，平均海拔在6000米以上的便有13座，称“太子十三峰”。主峰卡瓦格博海拔6740米，被藏族百姓誉为雪山之神，森林、草甸、冰川与奇花异草，是梅里雪山的宝藏。迄今为止，梅里雪山依然是从未有过人类登顶的处女峰。

Hutiao Gorge

The Majestic Force of the Yangtze River's First Gorge

虎跳峡 | 长江第一峡的千钧力量

Should the waves embody the formidable might of thunder and the valiant courage of ten thousand warriors, they would undoubtedly be the roaring torrents of the Hutiao ("Tiger Leaping") Gorge. At an elevation of 1,800 meters, the river's surface lies over 3,000 meters below the towering peaks, making it one of the world's deepest gorges. It is called this name because tigers and leopards can easily jump over at its narrowest point. Here, the Jinsha River flows southward from Shigu Town, carving a deep canyon between the Yulong and Haba Snow Mountains. Towering boulders obstruct the river's path, forcing the once-wide waterway into a sudden, narrow passage. The gorge's upper and lower ends span just 16 kilometers, with a vertical drop of 220 meters. Over a stretch of less than five kilometers, the river plummets more than 100 meters, its silt-laden waters forming colossal brown waves that churn violently. These waves race like a stampede of wild horses, filling the air with a deafening roar.

如果浪涛有雷霆万钧之势、万夫当关之勇，那么它一定是虎跳峡的滚滚惊涛。虎跳峡峡内江面海拔 1800 米，峰谷间高差达 3000 余米，是世界上最深的峡谷之一，因最窄处虎豹一跃即过，故得名虎跳峡。金沙江自石鼓镇南行，玉龙、哈巴两座雪山夹持而成深邃峡谷，巨石林立，阻挡一泻而下的江水，开阔的河道陡然狭窄，上峡口与下峡口相距仅 16 千米，落差 220 米，江水在不到 5 公里的地段内下跌百余米，江水挟裹着泥沙形成褐色滔天巨浪迂回而行，后浪追击前浪如同横冲直撞的万马，震耳欲聋。

Grand Canyon of the Nujiang River

A Hidden Mountain Sanctuary Amidst the Depths of Nujiang

怒江大峡谷 | 怒江深处的高山秘境

The roaring Nujiang River carves a majestic canyon running north to south through Nujiang Prefecture. Through the valley, a winding road follows the river's course, flanked by towering peaks. The dense, interwoven branches of the primeval forest form a thick canopy, while mountain mists blend with the river's waters, casting shifting patterns of shadow and light. Occasionally, indigenous people carrying bamboo baskets can be seen gliding across the river on zip lines. This canyon, arguably one of the world's most enigmatic, treacherous, and untouched, lies within the region of the Three Parallel Rivers of the Hengduan Mountains, stretching over 300 kilometers within Yunnan Province, with an average depth of 2,000 meters. Scattered along its banks are villages of the Lisu, Nu, Derung, Tibetan, and other ethnic groups. At its deepest point lies the quaint town of Bingzhongluo in Gongshan, where the canyon plunges to a depth of 3500 meters. Here, the Nujiang River takes on a gentle and serene demeanor. Just four kilometers south of Bingzhongluo, the river forms the "First Bend of the Nujiang River," a stark contrast to its otherwise imposing character. The terraced rice fields along the riverbank, with their orderly houses, exude a timeless tranquility, evoking a sense of a utopian paradise.

奔腾咆哮的怒江，在怒江州境内形成了一条南北走向的大峡谷，谷中公路沿江而行，两岸山峰连绵，原始森林盘枝交错密不透风，山岚弥漫江水，天色忽暗忽晴，江上偶尔划过背着背篓溜索过江的原住民。这条堪称世界上最神秘、最险奇和最原始的大峡谷，位于滇西横断山三江并流地带，在云南境内段长达 300 多公里，平均深度为 2000 米。在峡谷的两岸，散落着傈僳族、怒族、独龙族、藏族等少数民族的村寨。在峡谷最深处的贡山丙中洛小镇，谷深 3500 米，怒江到此却显得温柔和平静。丙中洛以南 4 公里处是与雄浑气质截然不同的“怒江第一湾”，江湾台地之上梯田层叠，房屋井然有序岁月静好，宛若桃源。

Three Parallel Rivers

A Natural Marvel Where Rivers Run Side by Side Yet Never Converge

三江并流 | 江水并流而不交汇

The Lancang, Jinsha, and Nujiang River basins cover an expansive area of 1.7 million hectares, capturing the essence of the Hengduan Mountains' rich biodiversity and geological features. This extraordinary region creates a rare natural spectacle where the three rivers flow side by side without converging, a phenomenon unparalleled anywhere else in the world.Originating from the Qinghai-Xizang Plateau, the Jinsha River, one of the main tributaries of the Yangtze River, rushes southward, carving its path through the rugged landscapes. As it passes through Lijiang, the river slices through towering mountains and deep valleys, making a breathtaking 180-degree turn at Shigu Town. Above this bend, lush rice paddies and neatly arranged villages create a picturesque scene. Historically, Shigu Town was a vital military stronghold, but today it is known for its scenic beauty. An ancient stone drum, inscribed by the Mu chieftain of Lijiang during the reign of Emperor Jiajing of the Ming dynasty (1522–1566), stands solemnly within the stone drum pavilion by the riverbank.

澜沧江、金沙江、怒江三江流域范围达170万公顷，几乎包含了横断山脉所有的生物和地质多样性的代表性样本，形成了世界上独一无二的“江水并流而不交汇”的奇特自然景观。而其中，作为长江的源头之水，金沙江自青藏高原出发，奔腾南行，在丽江境内高山峻岭间，在石鼓镇形成180度的急转弯。江湾之上，稻田优美、屋舍俨然；石鼓镇历来便是兵家必争之地，而今成为观景台。明嘉靖年间（1522—1566）由丽江木氏土司所刻的古石鼓仍旧萧肃安置于岸边石鼓亭内。

The Realm of Mortals and the Celestial Paradise

人间仙境 世外桃源

Lugu Lake

A Mysterious and Sacred Deep Lake on a Highland

泸沽湖 | 神秘圣洁的高原深湖

Lugu Lake, situated at the border of Yanyuan County in Sichuan's Liangshan Prefecture and Yunnan's Ninglang County, spans an area of approximately 50 square kilometers. The sunlight, filtered through the clouds, casts a soft glow, lending an ethereal clarity to the lake's colors. The surrounding trees, distant mountains, traditional Mosuo wooden houses, lakeside wildflowers, and the vibrant clothing of the locals harmonize with the ever-changing hues of the lake, imbuing the scene with a natural vitality and earthly charm.

泸沽湖，位于四川省凉山州盐源县与云南省宁蒗县交界处，湖泊面积约 50 平方公里。阳光透过云层的滤镜使得色彩增加了超凡脱俗的透明感，近树的远山、摩梭人的木屋、湖畔的野花、色彩斑斓的衣服与色彩变换的湖搭配在一起，又充满了人间的生机。

Xishuangbanna
Ecological Kingdom of the Tropical Rainforest

西双版纳 | 热带雨林的生态王国

Xishuangbanna is renowned as China's most pristine tropical ecosystem, earning it the titles of "Kingdom of Plants" and "Biological Gene Pool." Home to the country's only tropical rainforest nature reserve, this region is where the world's most radiant sunlight seems to gather, bathing the towering trees of the primeval tropical rainforest and the verdant rice fields of the countryside alike. The vibrant greenery beautifully complements the colorful traditional attire of the Dai people. Under the brilliant sun, the stilted houses in Dai villages shine with a deep, lustrous black.

西双版纳是中国热带生态系统保存最完整的地区，素有“植物王国”“生物基因库”之称，有中国唯一的热带雨林自然保护区。世间最明媚的阳光仿佛都集中在了西双版纳，无论是在林木高大的原始热带雨林，还是在乡间稻田，轻快的绿色与傣族五彩斑斓的服装色彩相映成趣；艳阳下，傣寨的吊脚楼散发着乌亮的光芒。

Shangri-La

A Utopian Dream in Every Traveler's Heart

香格里拉 | 旅人心中的乌托邦

Shangri-La, known in Xizang as "the sun and moon in the heart," sits at an average altitude of 3,459 meters and was formerly known as Zhongdian. When the winter snow melts in May, the vibrant colors of spring swiftly envelop every corner of this idyllic land. Scarlet rhododendrons burst into bloom along paths and valleys, while Bitahai Lake, cradled by towering coniferous forests and majestic mountains, awakens to embrace the year's most vigorous vitality.

The plateau breeze softly stirs, sending rhododendron petals drifting across the lake's surface, where they are mistaken for food by the fish, leading to the captivating scene known as "Fish Drunken by Rhododendron Petals." At this time of the year, the meadows and wetlands around Napa Lake are dressed in fresh greenery. Birds glide gracefully over the water, while herdsmen on horseback guide their flocks of sheep, gradually blending into the distant mountain ranges.

香格里拉藏语意为“心中的日月”，平均海拔3459米，原名“中甸”。五月冬雪融化，春色便迅猛地袭遍了香格里拉的每一处角落，红彤彤的杜鹃花怒放在每一条道路和山谷，被群山和高大针叶林所环抱的碧塔海也迎来一年中勃勃的生机。

高原之风拂过，杜鹃花瓣散落，游鱼误食后醉于湖面，形成了香格里拉最著名的“杜鹃醉鱼”奇观。此时纳帕海的草甸与湿地也焕发了新绿，飞鸟悠然滑翔过水面，牧民们骑着高头大马驱赶着羊群，渐行渐远，直到与山峦融为一体。

Yuanyang Rice Terraces

A Hani Ethnic Wonderland

元阳梯田 | 哈尼族的世外桃源

For over 1,300 years, the Hani people have harnessed the unique geographical and climatic conditions of the region to create this marvel of agrarian civilization. This awe-inspiring achievement spans across the four counties of Yuanyang, Honghe, Jinping, and Lyuchun, covering an area of approximately 1,000,000 mu (around 67,000 hectares), with around 170,000 mu (11,000 hectares) situated within Yuanyang County. The Hani people have resided in the Ailao Mountains for generations, passing down their agricultural wisdom and transforming wild rice into a staple crop, making them pioneers in early rice cultivation. In 2013, the Honghe Hani Rice Terraces were recognized as a UNESCO World Heritage site.

Mornings in Yuanyang Village are imbued with a serene, unmatched tranquility. As roosters crow, thin wisps of smoke rise from the tightly clustered Wa ethnic houses. Encircling the village are rice terraces, where the neatly arranged paddies and the reddish-brown soil of the Ailao Mountains blend into a harmonious tapestry. During the spring planting season, the fields shimmer with water; in summer, they are a lush green; and in autumn, they transform into a golden sea of ripened rice, filling the air with the rich aroma of harvest.

哈尼族1300多年来利用特殊地理气候创造了这片农耕文明奇观，它分布于元阳、红河、金平、绿春四县，总面积约100万亩，元阳县境内约计17万亩。哈尼族自古以来便生活在哀牢山内，他们世代传承农耕文化，成功驯化了野生水稻，因此成为人类早期驯化栽培稻谷的典范。2013年，红河哈尼梯田被成功列入《世界遗产名录》。

元阳村寨的清晨无比宁静，在鸡鸣声中，鳞次栉比的佤族房屋中冒出缕缕青色炊烟。村寨的四周，是层层叠叠的梯田，稻田与哀牢山泥土的红褐色有秩序地衔接，在春季播种时波光粼粼，夏季碧绿，秋季则是一片又一片沉甸甸的金黄色稻穗，散发着稻米香。

Dongchuan Red Land

Nature's Own Abstract Expressionist Painting

东川红土地 | 抽象派绘画的复刻

Nature's brush seems to have lavished special attention on Dongchuan, painting the landscape with bold strokes of red. Amid the hills and ravines of the Wumeng Mountains, a vivid tapestry of red earth emerges, interwoven with shades of deep red, light red, ochre, brownish-red, brick-red, and more.

Dongchuan Red Land is situated in the Dongchuan District of Kunming City, at an elevation of 1,800 to 2,600 meters. This distinctive landscape has formed under conditions of high temperatures and abundant rainfall. As soil interacts with the iron and aluminum-rich rainwater, oxidation occurs, gradually concentrating these elements. Over time, this creates a surface layer that is low in organic matter, highly acidic, and notably dense, resulting in the striking array of red hues that characterize the land.

大自然的画笔对东川仿佛格外关照，以浓重笔墨多涂抹了几笔红色，于是，乌蒙山的山丘沟壑之间，便在红土地上拼凑出一幅深红、浅红、赭红、棕红、砖红等颜色交错纵横的多彩画。

东川红土地位于昆明市东川区，海拔 1800 至 2600 米，因高温多雨发育而成，雨水中所富含的铁、铝成分在土壤中经过氧化慢慢沉积，达到一定比重，形成有机质少、酸性强、土质黏重的土地表层，进而形成了不同的红色。

Dawn and Dusk in the Ancient Cities

古城晨昏 人间烟火

Kunming

A Tranquil Ancient City Embraced by a Sea of Flowers

昆明 | 花海中的老城慢生活

Kunming, known as a city with eternal spring, is a place where the fragrance of flowers fills the air year-round. Every corner offers delightful cuisine, and the jacaranda trees stretch their branches along Qianwang Street. The lights of Nanping Pedestrian Street twinkle, while the agile fish dart through the waters of Green Lake. At Xishan, incense drifts from Huating Temple, and the waters of Dianchi Lake shimmer under the sun. Dianchi Lake, situated at the heart of the Kunming Dam, has been historically referred to as Kunming Lake. From late October to March, thousands of black-headed gulls embark on a long journey to its shores, spending the winter and nesting in the Caohai Wetland. Flocks of black-headed gulls soar fearlessly through the warm winter skies, where the lake and sky merge in harmony, creating a breathtaking spectacle.

四季如春的昆明，是空气中弥漫的花香、随处可见的美食、钱王街角伸出的蓝楹枝条、南屏步行街上的灯火、翠湖中灵巧的游鱼、西山华亭寺的香火以及水光潋滟的滇池。滇池位于昆明坝子中央，自古被称作昆明湖。每年 10 月下旬至次年 3 月，成千上万的红嘴鸥千里迢迢飞临滇池湖畔，在草海湿地内越冬繁衍后代。彼时冬日暖阳下，湖天一色，成群结队的红嘴鸥，漫天飞舞，毫不惧人，蔚为壮观。

The Ancient City of Dali

A Romance Between Mountains and Lakes

大理古城 | 山海之间的浪漫

As you stroll through the flower fields outside the ancient city of Dali, the towering Diancang Mountain rises majestically to the west, while the serene blue waters of Erhai Lake stretch out to the east. Between the mountain and the lake lies the ancient city, its timeless charm evident in the black-and-white eaves and gray-tiled roofs. In the narrow streets and alleys, the wind whispers through the trees, and magnolias bloom, enchanting the senses. The ancient city covers an area of approximately 3 square kilometers and enjoys a prime location. To the west, the main peak of Diancang Mountain, part of the Yunling Mountain Range, remains verdant year-round, with its highest summit, Malong Peak, standing at 4,122 meters and perpetually capped with snow. Erhai Lake, covering around 246 square kilometers, stands as the second-largest lake in Yunnan.

漫步在大理古城外的花田间，向西仰望，是巍峨的点苍山，向东眺望，是湛蓝沉静的洱海。山海之间，是古城老屋黑白相间的飞檐翘角、黛色屋瓦，街头巷尾，风吹树动，玉兰绽放，令人沉醉。古城占地约 3 平方公里，位置得天独厚。西侧点苍山云岭山脉南端的主峰，四季苍翠终年常绿，最高峰马龙峰海拔 4122 米，山顶终年积雪。洱海，湖水面积约 246 平方千米，是云南第二大湖。

Dayan Ancient Town

Poetic and Picturesque Hear of Lijiang Dam

大研古镇 | 丽江坝子的诗情画意

The gurgling stream is the lifeblood of Dayan Town. At dawn and dusk, its waters reflect the moonlight and sky, mirroring the lights and the exuberant and flourishing flowers along the banks. The stream weaves together rows of tiled houses, arched stone bridges, and the daily silhouettes of Naxi elders. The cheerful sound of the water mingles with the noises of washing and scrubbing, while the river carries the buttery aroma of Naxi baba, the scent of fresh coffee from new cafés, and the fragrance of ink from scholars' and poets' writings. Nestled in the heart of the Lijiang Dam, Dayan Town is embraced by Xiangshan Hill to the north, Jinhong Mountain to the east, and Shizi Hill to the west. These three mountains encircle the town, shielding it from the winter chills of the northwestern plateau. Therefore, even in the coldest months, the ancient town remains adorned with blooming flowers and flowing, unfrozen streams.

汩汩的溪流是大研镇的灵魂。晨昏里水影倒映着月色天光，倒映着两岸的灯火、热烈繁茂的鲜花，它串联起栉比的瓦屋、座座青石拱桥、纳西老人日复一日的身影，轻快的溪流声掺杂着捣衣声、洗刷声，河水上飘散着纳西粑粑的酥油香、崭新咖啡馆里的咖啡香，文人墨客的书墨香。大研镇位于丽江坝子的中央，镇北依象山、东靠金虹山、西枕狮子山，三山环抱，阻挡了来自西北高原的冬季寒流，使得古城内即便是在寒冷的冬季依然鲜花盛开、水流不冻。

Dukezong

A Nostalgic Echo of the Ancient Tea-Horse Road's Prosperity

独克宗 | 茶马古道的繁华追忆

The serene and ancient Dukezong Old Town, like a weathered elder, radiates majestic grandeur and carries a spirit that has witnessed the passage of countless journeys. “Dukezong,” meaning “castle built upon stones” or “Moonlight City,” once thrived as a bustling hub along the tea-horse trade routes connecting Yunnan, Sichuan, and Xizang. In its heyday, merchants from all directions converged here, creating an atmosphere of unparalleled vibrancy. The town’s old narrow alleys and ancient winding paths meander unpredictably, with large, smooth blue stones reflecting the faces of those who pass by. It feels as though the crisp sound of horse hooves still echoes through the centuries. Alongside these ancient paths stand Xizang-style houses, their wooden planks heavy and weathered, and their thick walls steadfast and resilient.

清冷的独克宗古城，似一位饱经风霜的长者，有着雄浑的气概和看尽千帆的气魄。“独克宗”，意为“建在石头上的城堡”“月光城”，曾为滇、川、藏茶马互市的要道通衢，当年四方商贾云集，可谓热闹非凡。城中的老巷古道，高高低低起伏不定，巨大青石光滑鉴人，仿佛能从风中倾听到数百年里风尘仆仆的清脆马蹄声。古道两侧的藏式老屋，木板沉重颜色老旧，围墙敦厚。

Heshun

An Artistic Fusion of Cultures in an Ancient Border Town

和顺 | 边陲古镇的混搭艺术

The misty haze of Baoshan Mountain adds a layer of mystery to Heshun Ancient Town, accentuating the timeless charm of its black-and-white walls and dark-tiled roofs. Known for its perpetual spring-like climate and gentle sunshine, the town was originally named Yangwendun, meaning "sun-warmed mound." During the reign of Emperor Kangxi of the Qing dynasty (1662–1722), it was renamed Heshun, meaning "harmony among officials and obedience from the people," inspired by the small river that meanders through the village. Later, during the reign of Emperor Zhengde of the Ming dynasty (1506–1521), the people of Heshun began venturing into Southeast Asia for trade. Over centuries of continuous development, Heshun evolved into a well-known hometown for overseas Chinese, developing a distinctive character and becoming a significant trading hub on both the Ancient Tea-Horse Road and the Southern Silk Road. Today, the town preserves more than a hundred century-old residences, along with ancestral halls, Buddhist and Daoist temples, stone bridges, archways, village gates, moon platforms, ancient pavilions, and old trees.

保山的山岚与氤氲，给和顺古镇平添了些许神秘，愈发衬托出那些黑白分明的粉墙黛瓦的厚重。因四季如春、阳光和煦，本被称为"阳温墩"，后清康熙年间（1662—1722）因小河穿村而过改名"河顺"，又取"士和民顺"之意更名为"和顺"。明正德年间（1506—1521），和顺人走出小镇到东南亚经商，经数百年不辍的建设，和顺成为如今风格迥然的著名侨乡，也成为茶马古道上和南方丝绸之路的贸易重镇。镇中留有上百所百年老宅，祠堂、寺院道观、石桥、牌坊、闾门、月台、古亭、老树等等保存完整。

Historical Relics and Cultural Heritage

古迹人文 精神家园

NSAU Bookstore of Librairie Avant-Garde

A Spiritual Haven Secluded in the Countryside

西南联大先锋书店 | 隐居乡间的精神栖息

The most poetic way to dwell is to steal moments of leisure under the sun in Yunnan, to engage in deep conversations about life's ideals at the foot of snow-capped mountains, or to savor a cup of tea while losing yourself in a book within a traveler's haven—a place where dreams converge, and a vast repository of knowledge nourishes the soul. This unique bookstore weaves itself into the cultural tapestry of Yunnan, preserving its spiritual legacy in places like Shaxi along the Ancient Tea-Horse Road, at the former site of the National Southwest Associated University by Nanhu Lake in Mengzi, within the Ming dynasty-built Chongzheng Academy in Weishan, and in the United Village of Shangri-La, as well as on the peak of Gaoligong Mountain. In these timeless spaces, new trees take root, shelves heavy with books stand tall, the rich aroma of coffee lingers in the air, vibrant attire of ethnic minorities catches the eye, and flowers bloom exuberantly outside the windows. A delicate crescent moon graces the night sky, with starlight softly illuminating the peaceful country paths.

最诗意的栖居，是在云南的阳光下偷闲、在雪山脚下畅谈理想，抑或在某座小镇上捧一杯茶、读一本书。先锋书店给怀揣梦想的旅者一处栖身之处，并敞开它万卷藏书的精神粮仓。在茶马古道上的沙溪，在蒙自南湖西南联大的旧址，在巍山建于明朝（368—1644）的崇正书院，在香格里拉联合村，在高黎贡山之巅，都是先锋书店与云南文化的融合与精神传承。沧桑的建筑角落是新植的绿树，琳琅满目的图书摆满四处，浓郁的咖啡飘香四溢，少数民族的花衣闪动，窗外花开酣浓，淡月如弦，星光璀璨照亮了淡淡乡间路。

Yunnan Provincial Museum

Unfading National Treasures

云南省博物馆 | 未褪色的国家宝藏

Yunnan Provincial Museum, established in 1951, finds its new home in the Guandu Ancient Town, where it graces the landscape under the clear blue sky. The museum's architecture reflects the traditional Yunnan residential style known as "Yike Yin ('One Seal')." Among its remarkable exhibits are the Lufengosaurus from the Early Jurassic period, dating back approximately 190 million years, and the Yuanmou Man from 1.7 million years ago. The museum also houses national treasures unearthed from ancient Yunnan tombs spanning from the Warring States Period (475-221 BCE) to the early Eastern Han Dynasty (25-220) at Lijiashan, including the bronze ox-tiger table and the gold-inlaid knight shell container from Shizhaishan, as well as Nanzhao art from the Dali Jianchuan Grottoes of the Nanzhao Kingdom, dating back to the Tang dynasty (618–907). These invaluable artifacts, all excavated from Yunnan, are significant highlights of the Yunnan Provincial Museum.

云南博物馆成立于 1951 年，新馆坐落于官渡古镇，仿云南传统民居样式“一颗印”造型矗立蓝天之下。从距今约 1.9 亿年的早侏罗纪时期的禄丰龙、距今 170 万年的元谋人，到古滇国李家山古墓［战国（前 475—前 221）至东汉（25—220）初期的墓葬］出土的国家宝藏牛虎铜案、石寨山出土国家宝藏鎏金骑士贮贝器、唐代（618—907）南诏国大理剑川石窟南诏艺术……这些都是云南出土的珍贵历史文物，也是云南省博物馆的重要展出内容。

Ganden Sumtseling Monastery

A Xizang Palace Along the Yunnan–Xizang Highway

噶丹松赞林寺 | 滇藏线上的藏式宫殿

The largest Xizang Buddhist monastery in Yunnan, often hailed as the "Little Potala Palace," is a majestic structure built into the mountainside, resembling an ancient fortress. Known as the "Museum of Xizang Art," this monastery offers a breathtaking panorama from its highest point. In the distance, ethereal snow-capped peaks rise above the horizon, while the outlines of distant towns and villages blur like wisps of smoke. Closer to view, the gilded rooftops of the Gzwa-tsang Main Hall, adorned with resplendent golden vases and roof tiles, shimmer in the sunlight. Vibrant prayer flags flutter in the wind, swaying between the sky and the monastery's yellow walls. The air resonates with the melodious chime of bells hanging from the eaves and the rhythmic chanting of sutras echoing from within the halls, creating an atmosphere of profound tranquility.

噶丹松赞林寺是云南最大的藏传佛教寺院，被誉为"小布达拉宫"。该寺依山而建，外形犹如一座古堡，有"藏族艺术博物馆"之称。在松赞林寺的最高处放眼望去，远处雪峰缥缈，城郭村庄如烟，近处扎仓大殿屋顶的鎏金宝瓶与金瓦夺目绚烂，五色经幡随风而动，在天空与黄色的围墙之间摇摆不停，耳中是屋檐四角垂吊的清脆铃声、殿中传来的阵阵经诵声，令心沉静。

Three Pagodas of Chongsheng Temple

A Retrospective Glance at the History of Nanzhao Kingdom and the Dali Kingdom

崇圣寺三塔 | 南诏与大理国的历史回眸

In the northern part of Dali Ancient City, nestled between the majestic Yingle Peak of Diancang Mountain and the tranquil waters of Erhai Lake, stand the Three Pagodas, reaching elegantly into the sky. The central pagoda, known as Qianxun Pagoda, is a quintessential example of architecture from the Tang dynasty (618–907), soaring to a height of 69.13 meters with its 16 tiers. It was constructed during the reign of Quanfengyou of the Nanzhao Kingdom (823–859). In ancient Dali, where marshlands and frequent floods were common, the royal family, during the reigns of Duan Zhengyan and Duan Zhengxing (1108–1172), erected two smaller pagodas in an architectural style inspired by the Song dynasty (960–1279), flanking the Qianxun Pagoda. These pagodas were constructed before the temple itself. Following the construction of Chongsheng Temple, nine of the twenty-two emperors from the Duan royal family chose to abdicate and embrace a monastic life here.

在大理古城北部，点苍山应乐峰与波平如镜的洱海之间，是挺拔耸立颜色圣洁的三塔，笔直入云。中间的千寻塔为典型的唐塔，高69.13米，共16级，为南诏劝丰佑时期（823—859）所建。大理古时沼泽与水患众多，段正严、段正兴时期（1108—1172）皇家又在千寻塔两侧建了两座宋代风格的小塔。先有塔后有寺，崇圣寺建成后，段氏家族22位皇帝中先后共有9位在此出家修行。

Yunnan Ethnic Village

A Diverse Cultural Family by the Shores of Dianchi Lake

云南民族村 | 滇池畔的大家庭

Along the riverbanks, winding country paths, towering mountains, and deep valleys, beneath banana trees, on snowy meadows, and within ancient towns and villages, the ethnic minorities of Yunnan infuse the landscape with vibrant hues, like a series of resplendent rainbows. Situated at Haigeng by Dianchi Lake, the Yunnan Ethnic Village brings together 25 ethnic minority communities. Here, you can find the stilted bamboo houses of the Dai, the "Three Rooms and One Screen Wall" homes of the Bai, the earthen homes of the Yi, and the patriarchal longhouses of the Jino, among others. Each village authentically represents the architectural styles, living customs, languages, and cultural elements of its respective ethnic group. The Ethnic Village celebrates a variety of ethnic festivals throughout the year, including the Bai's March Fair, the Dai's Water Splashing Festival, the Yi's Torch Festival, the Lisu's Knife Pole Festival, the Jingpo's Munao Zongge Festival, and the Naxi's Sanduo Festival. During these celebrations, villagers don their finest attire, singing and dancing with exuberance, creating a vivid tapestry of joy and harmony.

在河流溪畔、在乡间阡陌小路、在高山峡谷之中、在芭蕉树下、在雪山草甸、在老城古寨……少数民族的人们，是云南最绚烂多姿的一道道彩虹。集中了25个少数民族村寨的云南民族村位于滇池海埂。这里有傣族的吊脚竹楼、白族的“三坊一照壁”、彝族的土掌房、基诺族父系大长房，各少数民族的村舍建筑特点、生活习俗、文字语言均如实展示在此处。民族村结合各少数民族节日，在不同的时间举行白族的“三月街”、傣族的“泼水节”、彝族的“火把节”、傈僳族的“刀杆节”、景颇族的“目脑纵歌”、纳西族的“三朵节”等民族节日。届时，村民们身着盛装、欢声笑语、载歌载舞，展现出一幅幅欢乐祥和的画面。

雲南民族村

图书在版编目（CIP）数据

大美云南 ：汉英对照 / 陈曦著. -- 北京 ：五洲传播出版社，2024. 10. --（中国印象）. -- ISBN 978-7-5085-5282-8

Ⅰ. K297.4

中国国家版本馆CIP数据核字第20247LG124号

中国印象：大美云南

China Impressions：The Beauty of Yunnan

出 版 人：关　宏

责任编辑：杨　雪

助理编辑：汪梦琦

插　　画：玖玥工作室　王建华

文　　字：陈　曦

译　　者：潘英赵

审　　校：Lee Shee Yik

设计策划：山谷有魚

装　　帧：张伯阳

出版发行：五洲传播出版社

地　　址：北京市海淀区北三环中路 31 号生产力大楼 B 座 6 层

邮　　编：100088

发行电话：010-82005927，010-82007837

网　　址：http://www.cicc.org.cn，http://www.thatsbooks.com

印　　刷：北京市房山腾龙印刷厂

版　　次：2024 年 10 月第 1 版第 1 次

I S B N：978-7-5085-5282-8

开　　本：787mm × 1092mm　1/32

印　　张：6

字　　数：20 千

定　　价：49.8 元